Shakespeare Short Guides

Macbeth

notes and exemplar essays

E.N Cartwright

Copyright © 2023 E.N. Cartwright
All rights reserved.
979-8-3939-7866-2

DEDICATION

To my partner: the great listener.

CONTENTS

Acknowledgments	i
Introduction	Pg 3
Context	Pg 6
The Text Itself	Pg 8
The Plot and Characters	Pg 10
The Main Themes	Pg 14
Main Quotations	Pg 18
How to Write an Essay	Pg 24
Plagiarism	Pg 28
Exemplar Essay 1	Pg 29
Exemplar Essay 2	Pg 32
Exemplar Essay 3	Pg 35
Exemplar Essay 4	Pg 38
Exemplar Essay 5	Pg 41

ACKNOWLEDGMENTS

All my students, who have taught me as much for this as I have taught them.

Introduction

What's expected of me in this exam?

Well, hello, exam candidate.

I'm sure you've bought this purely to help you understand Shakespeare just a little better and not, of course, to cram an exemplar essay into your head a few days before the exam. Eek!

Now, the first thing to remember is that your teacher has given you specific advice for your exam, and she/he knows you much better than this book. So: FOLLOW THEIR ADVICE FIRST!

Do what they want you to do, take good notes, and listen to their feedback to improve. You have most likely had lots of attempts and feedback on your essay writing skills. Follow what your teacher wants you to do and use this guide to add to that.

Now, I have taught many kinds of exams to many pupils across many countries. Here is some general advice that I would bet applies to any exam:

- There is a time limit. It may be the essay is the only thing you need to do or part of a bigger paper, but you need to learn how to manage your time.
- You must write a complete essay – something half-finished scores less than a short but finished essay.
- You must show knowledge of the whole text (beginning, middle and end) to score top marks. A marker wants to

see that you understand it all.

- You must give **references** and **quotations**. These are the basis for any response.
- You should name **techniques** of English Lit (metaphor, simile, word choice, etc). This is usually in a mark scheme, looked for by markers.
- An introduction and a conclusion are rarely in the mark scheme but are expected in a longer piece of critical writing. If your exam doesn't call for a formal 'essay' then these may not to be needed but be guided by your teacher.
- The exam will usually provide a question/**task**. You usually choose just one question and it must be 'Drama' since you are covering Macbeth. Put the number of the question on your paper to help your marker.
- Don't write everything you know – choose what answers the task. Be selective, and just don't write a plot summary. That's not what a critical response is. Yes, show knowledge of what happens but a critical essay is something much more.
- The quickest way to do the above is to **repeat the key words** from the task itself. If it asks about a "character you feel sympathy for" then say the word "sympathy" at least twice a paragraph.
- There is no set 'way' to do an essay. You may have been taught TARTS, BAPs, PEAs, PEARs, PCQEs, and on and on, but it's rare for an exam board to have a preference.

  All these acronyms are just a teacher's way of trying to get you to do the following: show you know the play; show you know some quotations; show you know some analysis: and link all that information to the task give in the exam.

Macbeth

Context

Who was Shakespeare and why did he write this very violent play?

A writer whom English teachers love. He died a long time ago.

There's actually very little else you need to know about Shakespeare's actual life other than that usually. Most exams aren't testing you historical knowledge in any in-depth way. Why would an English Literature exam give you points for dates and faces? It wouldn't really.

That said, some exams have **social and historical context** in their mark scheme. This is where an understanding of the life and times of Shakespeare inform your essay. This information is the mark of a top band candidate, but even then the exam probably isn't looking for lists of facts. It is looking for your understanding of 'Macbeth' to be affected by information.

So ... after Queen Elizabeth 1st dies, King James 1st of England (son of Mary, Queen of Scots) ascends to the throne. We leave the Elizabethan era behind and enter the Jacobean era. This represents the unification of Scotland and England under one throne and a marked shift in culture for the people of this United Kingdom takes place as James is considered a 'weak' king.

King James 1 of England and Scotland comes from a long, long line of kings/queens who have been slaughtered or overthrown, making him afraid for his life. He feels that his throne can be taken away from, despite also believing that he has been placed there by God. There is a certain element of paranoia and fear for this king. This is made worse when he is the object of the Gunpowder Plot, an attempt to assassinate him by Catholics. As someone who (most definitely) had Catholic relatives, Shakespeare becomes worried that he may get arrested by the King. James 1st is also terrified of witches, witchcraft and the Devil. He seems to believe that the Devil is real, active in the world, and is a threat to the 'true' king (himself) placed there by God. In fact, James writes a rather famous manual for 'finding' and 'diagnosing' witches and demons called *Daemonologie*.

Shakespeare therefore decides to write a play to show King James that he is not threatening and a loyal servant. In this play, the plot of the witches fails (Macbeth fails to keep the throne) and Macbeth's **regicide** (the killing of a king rightfully placed on the throne by God) is punished by Macbeth being beheaded gruesomely. This is a clear attempt to flatter James 1st.

From this Shakespeare also gives a main theme which is worth considering: upsetting the natural order of the world causes calamity. Just as Macbeth kills the rightful king and the world begins to collapse, so the play acts as a warning to anyone thinking of killing King James. In this play, Shakespeare is overtly expressing his support of James and is publicly stating that King James is the rightful king of England and Scotland, placed there by God himself. This is known as the **divine right of kings**.

The play also includes several people who are (possibly) direct relatives of King James (such as Duncan and Banquo). Shakespeare deliberately changes history and makes them good, strong, righteous kings. This is a very deliberate attempt to stroke the ego of King James, a notoriously weak-willed King who was known as a coward and easily frightened. It made him feel good to know that his relatives could be seen in this light.

Therefore, 'Macbeth' could be seen as **propaganda** as it was written by Shakespeare to flatter King James.

The Text Itself
Remember it's a play!

Before we go much further you just need to remember one clear and distinct thing – this is a play/drama.

Why is that important?

Well, markers rarely see essays on Shakespeare that remember it is designed to be watched and not to be read. You get a few extra marks for understanding that idea. For example, acknowledging that there are actors, sets, special effects, stage directions, etc. These all show that you understand the **genre** of the thing that you have studied. This is rarely done and can make your essay stand out from the crowd.

These things also affect our understanding of the play. For example, many actresses can choose to play Lady Macbeth as powerful and dominating or as sly and manipulative – or both. Actors can choose to play Macbeth as ambitious and cunning or as mad and out of control – or both.

Directors can also make unusual choices to affect the play. Some directors stage 'Macbeth' so that it looks just like it would have in Shakespeare's time, but there are versions that set the play during World War 2 to emphasise that Macbeth is a soldier who has just been in a terrible battle.

Plays can change from how they are written basically!

Common mistakes because it's a drama:

- The person who wrote it is Shakespeare, the writer or the dramatist.

  It's **not** the poet or the maker, for example.

- The text is called the text, the play, or the drama.

  It is **not** the book or the film. You may have used a book or film to help you study the play, but you are writing an essay on the play.

- The audience or the viewer reacts.

  It is **not** the reader. You may have read sections of the play, but essays discuss influence on audience.

- You need to know the difference between **dialogue** and **stage directions**.

    - Dialogue: these are the words written on the page by Shakespeare and designed to be learned and said out-loud by the actors.

    - Stage directions: these are the instructions written by Shakespeare about sets, movement of actors, special effects.

      These are not meant to be reader to the audience, although you can analyse them in your essay.

      Shakespeare (because he directed his own plays) does not use many stage directions. He did not need to write many instructions down – he would just say them to the actors himself.

      Stage directions are usually printed on the page in *italics* to show their difference.

The Plot and Characters
Eh, what happens?

Now, this is a very complicated play. A lot happens but, to cheer you up a bit, you don't need to know every line and every 'why' and every action. The exam board do not expect you (a teenager!) to have knowledge which adults do not have – especially about some of the most complicated language written!

What they do expect is for you to have an overview understanding. They might not expect you to know what happens in Act 1 Scene 5 line 5, but they do expect you to know that Macbeth (spoiler alert!) dies at the end.

So, here's a basic overview ….

The Cast

- **Duncan**, king of Scotland at the start of the play
- **Malcolm** and **Donalbain**, Duncan's sons
- **Macbeth** and his wife **Lady Macbeth**
- **Banquo**, Macbeth's friend, and **Fleance**, his son
- **Three Witches**
- **Macduff,** Thane of Fife, and his family

'Back of the book' summary

A brave and apparently loyal Scottish general named Macbeth receives a prophecy from a trio of witches that one day he will become King of Scotland.

He becomes consumed by **ambition** and is dominated by his wife – leading to Macbeth murdering King Duncan, the rightful king of Scotland, to take the Scottish throne for himself.

He is then wracked with guilt and paranoia. Forced to commit more and more murders to protect himself, he soon becomes a tyrannical ruler.

Macbeth and Lady Macbeth soon descend into madness, and death is the punishment that awaits them for their destruction of the natural order of kings as laid out by God.

Act 1

Macbeth wins a great battle for King Duncan. The play starts with descriptions of the extreme violence that Macbeth is capable of – and praising his loyalty to his king.

On his ride home, he receives some **prophecies** (predictions about the future) from three witches – one of them is that he will get promoted to Thane of Cawdor and then become king. This seems unlikely to Macbeth, so he laughs them off. This sets up Macbeth's connection to the supernatural as well as his own ambition to be king.

When Macbeth's first promotion to Cawdor happens, he assumes that the witches are also correct in that he will be king. Macbeth and his wife decide the only way to make this happen is to kill King Duncan, who happens to be coming to visit.

But the witches also predicted that Banquo's son would be king … That hints that Macbeth will never have kids/be overthrown by Banquo's children.

Act 2

Macbeth kills Duncan while he is sleeping after much deliberation because what he is doing is evil – and worse than just evil as he is killing God's anointed king. Macbeth is deliberately setting himself in opposition to all that is good and holy in the world.

When Duncan is discovered dead, everyone is basically very suspicious of Macbeth from the very beginning, and Duncan's sons run away.

Act 3

Macbeth begins to unravel. There are many possible reasons why (guilt, PTSD as a warrior, and he hasn't slept in days) but paranoia sets in – so he sends some murderers to kill Banquo and his son as Macbeth fears the other prophecies of the witches. They kill Banquo but fail to kill the boy.

Macbeth then holds a banquet to celebrate his coronation where he sees the ghost of Banquo sitting at a table. He basically starts to go mad, confessing to his crimes in public. Lady Macbeth manages to control him and get him out before he damages their situation further.

Act 4

Macbeth visits the witches again and receives some more prophecies – this time that he can't be killed by any man "of woman born" and that he is safe until Birnam Wood comes to Dunsinane Hill. This makes Macbeth imagine that he is invincible as these two things seem impossible.

Macbeth is now seeking out the witches – and, therefore, the Devil – in this scene. This is a further crime in the eyes of Shakespeare's audience. Macbeth is descending into immorality and evil, driven by his ambition to be king and keep the throne.

Act 5

Phew – nearly there! But this is a long one ...

Lady Macbeth delivers her most famous speech ("out damn'd spot") during the sleep-walking scene. Destroyed by guilt and a lack of sleep, she kills herself. This is in stark contrast to the strong and powerful figure who has dominated other parts of the play. In places she seemed to almost to control Macbeth and, in fact, she is often 'blamed' for much of the early violence in the play. This scene represents her punishment and descent into evil and madness.

We do not see this death on stage, only hear it reported to Macbeth. This causes Macbeth to fall into despair and deliver his most famous speech: "Tomorrow and tomorrow and tomorrow" which is about the brevity of life.

Earlier in the play, Macbeth ordered the murder of Macduff's family (a man loyal to Duncan and his sons). Macduff has returned with an English army to overthrow the new king of Scotland, considered an evil tyrant. The army has made weapons from the trees at Birnam Wood and are now marching on Dunsinane Hill. This seems to be fulfilling the prophecies of the witches and Macbeth begins to feel fear.

The battle ends with a challenge between Macduff and Macbeth. Right up until almost the very end, Macbeth feels protected by the witches and feels invincible. He brags out-loud he can't be killed by a man "of woman born".

Well, Macduff was 'born' by Caesarean section – 'cut' out of the womb rather than born in the traditional way. This is an example of **literary quibble**. The witches told a version of the truth to Macbeth to make him feel he was invincible when, all along, they knew Macduff would kill him.

Which is what happens.

Macduff kills Macbeth – and eventually Banquo's descendants become kings (specifically James 1).

Main Themes
Yeah, but what is it all about?

A theme is an idea or message crafted by the writer (or rising out of the text) that engages the audience to think. It is an idea or message not just about the events or characters, but something wider – it is a philosophical, social or moral point about the whole world or society.

It is often linked to the 'message' of the play or what the audience is supposed to 'learn from' the play. These aren't exactly what a theme are, but they are a good starting point to begin to wrap your head around what it is.

Ultimately, it is the 'point' of the play; the thing we, the viewer, are supposed to 'take' away from having watched it.

Themes are important parts of texts – but are difficult!

Understanding of theme is important if you are looking to enter those top bands and get those top grades. Thematic understanding – and theme-based essays – allow you to discuss the 'big ideas' of the text and, therefore, allow you to show how smart you are.

It is also in the mark scheme. What you have learned/taken away from the text (what has stuck with you) is part of the mark scheme. We usually acknowledge this in the conclusion, sometimes as simple as "This drama has taught me that …" and then we discuss a major theme **relevant to task**.

Theme 1: ambition

The question Shakespeare poses to us is: how far should we allow ambition to control us? Macbeth's ambition pushes him to committing acts of true evil.

Shakespeare, therefore, seems to be telling the audience to curb and control ambition, that it is a negative force that needs to be controlled.

Theme 2: the natural order

Shakespeare presents a world where the natural order is disrupted. The witches, creatures of evil and chaos, manipulate the situation so that Macbeth kills the 'rightful' king. This causes disruption to many of the natural elements of the play, such as the weather and the ability to sleep.

Shakespeare, therefore, seem to be showing the audience that there is a natural order to the world that should not be disrupted. This is specifically important to James 1 who wants the divine right of kings to be respected as the natural order.

Theme 3: appearances vs reality

Lady Macbeth encourages Macbeth a number of times to appear good when he is really plotting evil. Macbeth also tries to pretend to be one thing to the court when he is really another. As the drama goes along, Macbeth's ability to keep up this pretence collapses and he reveals himself a tyrant. Macbeth's madness reveals the truth of him to the audience.

Shakespeare, therefore, seems to be teaching the audience that appearances are deceptive and that they cannot be maintained – that reality will always come through to the surface despite our best attempts to hide what is really underneath it all.

Theme 4: guilt

Macbeth and Lady Macbeth are slowly taken over by their guilt. As the play goes along, it consumes them. Lady Macbeth especially is consumed by her guilt, resulting in an inability to sleep and a rising madness. Lady Macbeth, in fact, tries to claim that guilt is something that can be ignored or washed away – but then she is proved wrong by her own death later in the play.

Shakespeare, therefore, seems to be teaching the audience that guilt is a force to be reckoned with.

Theme 5: masculinity

Macbeth is a renowned solider and, in fact, the play begins with detailed descriptions of his violence and actions towards other. He is held up as an example of masculinity. Yet this extreme violence and masculinity is used against him by Lady Macbeth. She manipulates him (calling him weak, not a real man) when she wants him to kill Duncan. She uses his masculinity against him, emasculates him to exert power over him.

Shakespeare is unlikely to mean this theme overtly, but a message of the drama does seem to be that masculinity is a toxic force when left unchecked.

Theme 6: free will and fate

Macbeth is given a number of prophecies by the witches. What's really going to make you scratch your head is the question: would Macbeth have killed Duncan if the witches hadn't predicted it? Was Macbeth always destined to kill the king or did he only do it because he *thought* he should?

Shakespeare, therefore, isn't presenting us with a clear fact. He is, instead, presenting us with the idea of fate and leaving it open to us, as an audience, to decide for ourselves if it exists.

Theme 7: sleep

Both Macbeth and Lady Macbeth report an inability to sleep after killing Duncan. At the time of Shakespeare, a lack of sleep is both a sign of being a witch and also a curse from the Devil. Their lack of sleep indicates their association with evil. But, interestingly, a modern audience would understand the devastating effects a lack of sleep has on people – it causes hallucinations and erratic behaviour, as displayed by Macbeth and Lady Macbeth.

Shakespeare, therefore, presents sleep as a place that reveals truth and its importance to humans.

Theme 8: power

Macbeth represents the corrupting influence of power. Macbeth's desperation to hold on to power influences him to killing children and taking action that is truly evil. This is related to the diving right of kings – he was not chosen by God, he is not designed to be able to hold 'power' without it destroying him.

Shakespeare, therefore, is teaching the audience that power is only for a select few, that it destroys when it is in the wrong hands.

Theme 9: betrayal

Macbeth betrays Duncan, Banquo and Macduff. Macbeth is betrayed by those who claim to be loyal. Lady Macbeth is betrayed by herself, confessing to her crimes in her sleep. Betrayal winds its way throughout the play. Betrayal is a force that cannot be stopped inside the play.

Shakespeare, therefore, is teaching the audience that humanity is defined by betrayal, that it is an inescapable force in human nature. It is something that is inherent in all humanity we must be vigilant against becoming a betrayer.

Main quotations
Some of the big quotes and analysis

This is a play that is packed full of 'quotes' that you could learn and analyse. There is no real way – or real need – to cover every single quotation. I have chosen what, to me, seem the most important and the ones most relevant to an exam.

Since you are probably thinking of writing an essay, the quotes are arranged chronologically from beginning to end. This allows you to choose quotes from the beginning, middle and end of the play – the exam board wants to see this. Any good essay will have **coverage** of the whole text, not just one part.

Each quote is also labelled with what **tasks** it will be useful for, for example what themes it discusses or what character it reveals. This will allow you to start thinking not just about analysis of quotes, but also how they might be used in order to answer a question in essay format.

Much of the analysis you will find here is 'commonly accepted' (i.e. most people would agree that this is what these lines mean or why they were written) but there is always room for your own ideas or differing interpretations.

You may have studied one of these quotations in your classroom and your teacher may have taught you something different – even the opposite – but the beauty of Shakespeare lies in the complexity ... there's room for multiple answers!

Act 1

"Fair is foul, and foul is fair"

(The Witches, Act 1 Scene1)

The witches are discussing the good weather (*"fair"*) versus the terrible events of the battle (*"foul"*)., something done by Lady Macbeth later in the play using very similar words. They are also establishing their own opposition to societal norms – what humans see as *"fair"* the witches see as *"foul"*, and what humans see as "foul" the witches see as *"fair"*.

But Shakespeare is also discussing the difference between appearances and reality (between seeming good and being evil or looking ugly but being good). It establishes, right at the beginning, that you cannot trust what you see on the stage.

It is also a very simple line that, when you investigate it, is almost confusing and strange. Shakespeare is establishing a world where even language is in a state of confusion.

Tasks: the witches; supernatural; appearances vs reality

"Stars, hide your fires! Let not light see my black and deep desires"

(Macbeth, Act 1 Scene 4)

Macbeth has heard the prophecies of the witches and they have sparked his ambition, his *"black and deep desire"* to be king. Macbeth knows the quickest (and perhaps only) route to this is to kill Duncan, a thought that he should not be having as he is supposed to be the loyal general of the king.

This is one of many repeated references to *"black"* and being hidden. Macbeth wants to *"hide"* his actions from the *"stars"* (i.e. heaven and God). He wants to do his deeds unseen and in secret – both because he doesn't want found out but also because he cannot face who he really is.

Tasks: Macbeth; ambition; guilt; appearances vs reality

*"Come, you spirits, that tend on moral thoughts! unsex me here,
And fill me from the crown to the toe, top-full Of direst cruelty"*

(Lady Macbeth, Act 1 Scene 5)

Lady Macbeth has heard of the prophecies and has decided she and Macbeth will kill Duncan. She gives a monologue where she is working herself up, trying to give herself courage to match her ambition. In this section she even seems to want to change gender ("*unsex me here*") as she feels being a 'weak' woman doesn't suit her inner strength and power. Yet, she strangely doesn't necessarily want to be a man – she seems to be weaving a spell ("*spirits*") and does seem to want to be a powerful witch ("*direst cruelty*"). Being a man isn't powerful enough for her.

This establishes the power and evil of Lady Macbeth from the very beginning. If these are her intentions, then it is interesting to note that by the end of the play she asks for the opposite! She tries to hide from the guilt of what she has done, whereas here she seems to be desperate to become evil.

Tasks: Lady Macbeth; ambition; supernatural; power

"Look like the innocent flower, But be the serpent under it."

(Lady Macbeth, Act 1 Scene 5)

Lady Macbeth tries to 'sweet talk' Macbeth into committing regicide and killing Duncan. She knows that Macbeth sort-of wants to already and she is just talking him round to his own ambition. In this scene it is very clear that Lady Macbeth has abandoned societal expectations (that she be a good wife, meek, subservient to Macbeth and her king) whereas Macbeth is still trying to look like he is holding onto his role as a loyal subject.

Lady Macbeth is very overt her about hiding ("*look like*"/"*but be*") and references the devil ("*the serpent*"). Serpents also have 'forked tongues' (a metaphor for lying and being manipulative) which is exactly what Lady Macbeth is doing!

Tasks: Lady Macbeth; ambition; appearances vs reality

Act 2

"Is this a dagger which I see before me, The handle toward my hand?"

(Macbeth, Act 2 Scene1)

One of Macbeth's most famous lines! He is on his way to kill Duncan and feels like a supernatural force is pulling him forward. Now it is possible that a special effect could be used on stage to make a 'dagger' appear (which hints the witches have created an illusion) or it could be staged so that Macbeth is clearly seeing nothing (which hints he is beginning to go mad).

The fact that Macbeth phrases it as a question shows his confusion and the lack of reality and stability. You can't trust your eyes here. The phrase *"handle toward my hand"* is interesting because it seems to imply that Macbeth feels like some outside force is compelling his actions – he is fated to do what he is about t do. This allows Macbeth to avoid guilt because it isn't really his 'fault'.

Tasks: Macbeth; guilt; supernatural; fate; ambition

Act 3

"I am in blood steepp'd in so far, that, should I wade no more, returning were as tedious as go o'er."

(Macbeth, Act 3, Scene 4)

Macbeth is contemplating the murders he has committed – and the further murders he must commit. Here he compares these murders to being in water (*"wade"*). It implies there's so much blood that he is walking in it – literally knee deep.

The quotation implies that Macbeth's actions have so much momentum and he has done so much (*"steepp'd in so far"*) that to stop (*"wade no more"*) or go back to his old life (*"returning"*) would be too difficult (*"tedious"*). It is easier to keep killing.

Tasks: Macbeth; ambition.

Act 4

"Double, double toil and trouble; Fire burn and cauldron bubble"

(Witches, Act 4, Scene 1)

Another incredibly famous line from the play, often repeated and referenced. Macbeth – no longer sleeping and losing his mind – goes back to the witches to consult with them. This was a crime in the Jacobean era as it is consulting the devil.

The witches are creating a magic brew and spell, speaking in rhyming couplets to create a singsong like effect. It makes the language both very simple but hard to understand. It makes them seem child-like, threatening and inhuman. It's the Shakespearean equivalent of when the little child sings in the horror film – you know something bad is going to happen!

The most important element here is word choice and repetition. The word "*double*" is double repeated, showing the importance of doubles. It represents that the witches' words have two meanings (one that Macbeth wants, and the truth), but also represents the play is full of 'double', false or fake people.

The play also uses doubles an awful lot. Some of the characters can represent doubles or shadows for Macbeth. For example,

- Banquo is Macbeth's 'loyal' double, doing the things that Macbeth should have done when they first encountered the witches.
- Lady Macbeth can be seen as his dark 'double' or shadow, pushing him and his ambition along the path of evil.
- King Duncan is an oppositional 'double' – the opposite kind of king that Macbeth turns out to be.

Overall, this seemingly small and simple line has a great deal of depth and meaning to the play. But the line is so childish sounding that the meaning is lost on Macbeth – who most needs to understand it.

Tasks: Macbeth; witches; supernatural; appearances vs reality

Act 5

"Out, damned spot! Out, I say!"

(Lady Macbeth, Act 5, Scene 1)

Lady Macbeth starts to sleepwalk and talks in sleep. This is her guilt for killing Duncan and her part in Macbeth's tyranny. In front of doctor (sent by Macbeth) and her ladies in waiting, she obsessively washes invisible blood from her hands in her sleep and confesses to murder.

The *"damned"* is ironic as she is now damned to Hell for her part in killing the king. It is also ironic because she seemed, earlier in the play, to wish to be associated with the Devil and witchcraft but she now regrets it. The *"out"* refers to the blood that she can see on her hands but is also the metaphorical stain of sin that she now carries with her. She wants to return to being 'pure' and 'good' – and 'clean'.

The sentences here are short, ending in exclamation. These are some of the most emotional and least complex sentences that she uses, showing the descent and change in her mind since the start of the drama.

Tasks: Lady Macbeth; guilt; ambition; sleep

"Life's but a walking shadow, a poor player that struts and frets his hour upon the stage, and then is heard no more. It is a talk told by an idiot, full of sound and fury, signifying nothing"

(Macbeth, Act 5, Scene 4)

After the death of Lady Macbeth – but before his own death – Macbeth gives a very famous speech in which he shows he has lost all hope. He believes that God is an *"idiot"* and life is a *"poor player"*. He sees life as pointless (*"signifying nothing"*) and full of only pain (*"full of sound and fury"*).

Yet still his ambition drives him on to his battle with Macduff – he has come too far to stop now.

Tasks: Macbeth; fate; ambition

Writing an essay

Yeah, but how do I write an essay?

Okay, well, let's start with the fact that your teacher has probably taught you some structures already, and you've probably practised it since you were in your first years of senior school! You know how to write an essay – all that knowledge is tucked away in your brain somewhere. Even if you are not being asked to write an essay, you know how to write analytically!

But if you need a little reminder, here's some advice….

Task

The exam paper has a task on it. This is what is going to drive your essay. You should be referring to that task twice in every paragraph of your essay. We usually use the **key word from the task** in the first line and last line of each paragraph. This is called 'topping and tailing' – it is at the top and tail of each paragraph. This lets the marker know that you are definitely answering the question/doing the task.

Do not just write all the information that you know. Only write information that is relevant to the task. For example, if you decide to write about Macbeth's ambition – why are you talking about Lady Macbeth's suicide? You may know about it, but it probably isn't full relevant! This loses marks.

Introductions

These are not explicitly in many mark schemes (although "structure" often is and introductions are structure), but they are expected by markers. They allow the marker to understand the task, text and approach you are going to take. They set the scene, set up the essay, give the marker the low down, etc, etc.

There are standard things introductions contain:
- **Title in inverted commas:** "Macbeth"
- **Full name of author:** William Shakespeare
- **Reference to task:** I am going to discuss …
- **Some sort of summary:** "Macbeth" is about

Weaker introduction

Task: discuss a drama where there is a character you dislike.

I am going to discuss "Macbeth" by William Shakespeare. I am going to talk about the character of Lady Macbeth and why I dislike her. This play is about Macbeth, a man who kills a king and takes over. It is set in Scotland. He dies at the end, and Lady Macbeth also kills herself.

Better introduction

Task: discuss a drama where there is a character you dislike.

William Shakespeare's "Macbeth" is a drama where one the central characters, Lady Macbeth, inspires loathing and deep dislike in the audience. She and her husband, Macbeth, kill Duncan, King of Scotland. But their ambition drives them towards committing ever great acts of evil, finally causing their mental, spiritual and literal downfall. Lady Macbeth, by the end of the drama, obsessively washes unseen blood from her hands to revoke her own guilt – and committing suicide. I shall discuss how Shakespeare builds such a dislike-able character.

Analytical paragraphs

These are the paragraphs that make up the **body** of your essay. This is mostly what your marks are going to come from. You need to make sure you have a minimum of three – one from the start, one from the middle and one from the end. This shows coverage. You probably want to work **chronologically** (start to middle to end) rather than out of order.

You may have been taught an acronym (PEA, PEAR, PCQE, etc) for producing these. These systems do work. I am going to speak more generally, and you should see it's the same information I'm telling you – just different terminology.

The standard things included in analytical paragraphs:

- **A literary technique:** The writer uses a simile
- **Reference to the task:** This creates dislike
- **A quotation in " " marks**: "Out, damned spot!"
- **Knowledge of the drama**
- **Analysis of the quotation**

Weaker analytical paragraphs

Task: discuss a drama where there is a character you dislike.

Shakespeare uses an exclamation, "Out, damned spot!" This is from the end when Lady Macbeth is washing her hands. It shows she feels guilt. This makes me dislike her because she's bad.

Better analytical paragraphs

Task: discuss a drama where there is a character you dislike.

Shakespeare uses an effective exclamation, "Out, damned spot!" in Act 5 Scene 1 during Lady Macbeth's famous hand washing scene. The exclamation shows the depth of her guilt, while "damned" shows her anger at her mental state but ironically references her own "damned" soul. The audience dislike her action and emotion but may feel sympathy for her situation.

Conclusions

Like, introductions, these are not always explicitly in the mark scheme (again "structure" usually is and conclusions are a point of structure), but are expected by markers. They summarise your ideas, round off your essay, give you a last chance to say anything to show a lesson that you have learned.

There are standard things conclusions contain:
- **Concluding phrase:** In conclusion,
- **Repeat in inverted commas:** "Macbeth"
- **Repeat full name of author:** William Shakespeare
- **Reference to task:** I have discussed …
- **Personal reaction:** I have learned …

Weaker conclusion

Task: discuss a drama where there is a character you dislike.

In conclusion, I have discussed "Macbeth" by William Shakespeare. I have talked about the character of Lady Macbeth and why I disliked her. I didn't like her because of all the evil things that she did. I have learned not to be like her.

Better conclusion

Task: discuss a drama where there is a character you dislike.

In conclusion, William Shakespeare's "Macbeth" was a drama driven by the ambition of the central characters. This ambition reveals the depth of Lady Macbeth's dark soul, exposing her to the dislike of the audience. Yet her ability to embrace this dislike and evil gives her some power within the play. The drama does set up her punishment, showing the audience the Godly punishment for her hubris and actions. Shakespeare uses her to leave a clear message: do not over-reach, and that the natural order must be maintained … tampering with it causes chaos!

Disclaimer about the use of exemplars:

Exemplars are useful ways to 'see' what high end essays look like and understand what to sound like when you write your own. It can even be useful to try to memorise parts or ideas from an exemplar to write in your exam!

You fully have my permission to use these exemplars to *inform* your own work, and as revision/learning tools for an exam. That's what they were created for.

But **plagiarism** is never acceptable.

This is trying to pass off an exemplar as piece of homework or claiming that you have written it when you did not. Especially when that work forms part of a grade awarded to you by a teacher.

Your teacher will know! Don't be a fool!

Exemplar Essay 1
Discuss a drama with an interesting character.

William Shakespeare's "Macbeth" is a drama which presents to the audience an interesting main character, specifically Lady Macbeth who seems in conflict with herself and society. This drama concerns the actions of the Thane Macbeth and his wife as the witches lead them to committing the Jacobean sin of regicide and, after this action, both characters then suffer a psychological break down which ultimately leads to their deaths. This essay will focus on the character of Lady Macbeth who feels trapped between society's expectations of women and her own ambitions – creating an impact on the drama overall.

To begin, the writer uses a command in Act 1 Scene 5 to begin describing Lady Macbeth in her first appearance, "[c]ome, you spirits that tend on mortal thoughts, unsex me here", after she has received a letter from Macbeth detailing the prophecies of the witches. During her soliloquy, Lady Macbeth realises she and Macbeth must kill Duncan to progress in their ambition and is trying to talk herself into this evil action. She seems committed to this from the beginning. The phrase "unsex me" implies that Lady Macbeth wishes to be transformed from the weak woman she feels now into something more powerful and evil. It implies that, internally, she feels more like a man and wishes to gain this power. She is unhappy being a woman. But the word "unsex" could hint that she wishes to lose gender all together and become something monstrous and powerful – like a witch. She is even resorting to casting a spell ("come"/"spirits") and speaking to the devil, a crime in the Jacobean era. The writer effectively shows the audience Lady Macbeth's conflict within herself – that there is a mismatch between her appearance and gender with her ambition and hopes. There seems to be a disconnect for Lady Macbeth and she is suffering an internal conflict, creating an interesting and compelling character from the outset.

The writer then uses a question in Act 1 Scene 7 to show the power of Lady Macbeth, "Art thou afeard to be the same in thine own act and valor as thou art in desire?" Here Lady Macbeth attempts to encourage and goad Macbeth into killing Duncan, the king, by appealing to his ambition and attacking his masculinity. The word "afeard" shows us that Lady Macbeth considers Macbeth's reluctance to kill his cousin, the king, as a kind of weakness that she holds against him, seen when she also calls him a "coward" later. This is ironic considering he is a solider and this is a direct challenge to his masculinity, which she hopes will anger and provoke him into action. She seems very manipulative and in control of her husband here. Lady Macbeth here implies she sees no difference between "act" and "desire", implying that she is strong and ambitious enough to get what she wants, but that Macbeth is too "afeard" to cross that divide. Lady Macbeth, in this scene, represents unbridled and uncontrolled ambition, acting like the 'devil on Macbeth's shoulder' encouraging him to his deepest, darkest desires. Her alignment with the witches from earlier in Act 1 is complete here. This very effectively conveys to the audience the drive and power that Lady Macbeth has, with even her sentence structures (the question) attempting to provoke Macbeth (into answering, into a response, into action). This creates an interesting if unlikeable character that the audience is intoxicated with.

In Act 5 Scene 1, the writer then shows us a huge change in Lady Macbeth through the use of imagery, "what's done cannot be undone". This is towards the close of the play during Lady Macbeth's sleep walking scene. Together they have killed Duncan and Macbeth has slaughtered the family of Macduff, which causes

Lady Macbeth to have a psychological break down and obsessively start washing her hands ("out damn'd spot"). Lady Macbeth's complex language (her main power) has descended into simple phrases like "done" and into simple repetitions. Her ambition and drive is replaced by regret, with the word "cannot" implying that she has tried to change what she has done but she is unable to. She regrets her actions and her ambitions. Much of her strength and power was, in fact, façade and that has collapsed now to reveal only a broken woman. Lady Macbeth, by the end of the play, seems psychologically broken down and beaten, a huge contrast to the figure at the start who told Macbeth "what's done is done" as advice for forgetting their actions. This sentence also ironically recalls earlier in the play when Lady Macbeth had said that a "little water" could wash them both clean of the murder – well no amount of water she applies now will wash away the 'stain' of her sin. This hallucination that Lady Macbeth experiences could be sent from the witches as a curse or a punishment from God, while a modern audience would read this is Obsessive Compulsive Disorder (OCD) and delusions brought on by her psychological stress. The writer effectively shows an interesting collapse in the character of Lady Macbeth and a huge change in her.

    In conclusion, William Shakespeare's "Macbeth" is a play with an interesting main character who has a huge impact on the play as a whole. Lady Macbeth is much of the driving force behind the start of the play due to her desire for power – and to break out of the role of a 'trapped; Shakespearean woman – and her manipulations of her husband. This results in many deaths and, ultimately, in her own psychological break down. One could argue that she deserves the fate that she ends up with – her suicide – but we could feel some sympathy for this ambitious, clever woman trapped in her time. The main lesson to be taken from Lady Macbeth's downfall is around hubris and ambition – that often our deepest desires should remain only a desire. We should be careful – and perhaps fear – what we most want.

Exemplar Essay 2

Discuss a drama with an important relationship.

William Shakespeare's "Macbeth" is a drama in which there is an important relationship worthy of discussion due to its impact on the play as a whole, namely that between Macbeth and his wife, Lady Macbeth. This drama concerns the actions of the Thane Macbeth and his wife Lady Macbeth with the witches leading them to committing the Jacobean sin of regicide and, after this action, both characters then suffer a psychological break down which ultimately leads to their deaths. This essay will focus on the relationship between these characters and the impact that this relationship has upon the drama as a whole, namely how it drives their ambition to deeper and darker places.

    To begin, the writer uses a metaphor in Act 1 Scene 5, "[y]et I do fear thy nature: it is too full o' th' milk of human kindness", when Lady Macbeth has just received a letter from Macbeth detailing the prophecies of the witches. It is interesting Lady Macbeth is the first individual Macbeth 'tells' about the prophecies, showing his trust and love – referring to her as his "partner". But during her soliloquy, Lady Macbeth realises she and Macbeth must kill Duncan to progress in their ambition. Yet the word "kindness" shows us Lady Macbeth's vision of her husband as a good man, which she feels will get in their way of killing Duncan. She turns something seen as a positive into a negative in her eyes (a weakness), which links to "fair as foul" from earlier. The word "milk" is ironic here as she implies that Macbeth is womanly – linking to breast milk – implying she feels she is more masculine than her husband, with more ambition and will to carry out what must be done. This is a major theme before the death of Duncan. The writer effectively sets up the dynamic between Lady Macbeth and Macbeth – there is a love between these two characters, but Lady Macbeth considers herself the 'strong' and dominant personality within their relationship. It is especially ironic that Lady Macbeth thinks, from the audience's perspective, as Act 1 before this has been dominated by descriptions of how destructive and powerful Macbeth is as a solider – something Lady Macbeth never quite sees. The reality of war and death is something that only comes to her once Duncan has died.

The writer then uses an order to further develop this relationship during the death of Duncan, "Infirm of purpose! Give me the daggers!" This is Lady Macbeth's order to Macbeth just after he has killed Duncan but fails to follow their plan correctly because he has brought the daggers with him rather than leaving them there. Macbeth's confused action shows the importance of the incident and its effect on him – he seems distracted and unable to focus, almost as if he doesn't care if he is caught. This contrasts with Lady Macbeth's "give me", which shows her practicality and her seeming power – she is focused only on the plan and not the moral implications of their actions. She seems cold and unaffected, unlike Macbeth, and like she is capable of anything – something that she stated earlier, saying she would kill her own child for this ambition.. She also chastises Macbeth ("infirm of purpose") implying, again, that he is weak and unstable, which is truly ironic since he has just killed Duncan. This could just be another way for Lady Macbeth to gain power over him by verbally lowering him and raising herself (you are weak, I am strong), something she does throughout the play. This seems to reinforce the established relationship between Macbeth and his wife, where she verbally seems to be colder and more ambitious than her husband. She also seems emotionally void to her actions – but, as the plan unfolds, the disconnect between Lady Macbeth's words and her emotional state are revealed.

In Act 5 Scene 5, Shakespeare uses imagery to show how this relationship then comes to a close and affects the whole play, "she should have died hereafter". This is Macbeth's reaction to being told that Lady Macbeth has killed herself by throwing herself from the castle walls. This is the beginning of his famous "tomorrow" speech about the pointlessness of life. This particular line has a number of interpretations, depending upon how the actor/director 'play' the line and what you think of Macbeth. There is ambiguity on the word "hereafter" – it could mean she would have died anyway and he doesn't care, or it could mean that she should have died "after" the battle but lived a long life first. The sentence could mean that by this point in the play their relationship has totally collapsed and he doesn't care at all, or it could imply that her death is so devastating that he cannot imagine life without her. This affects how we understand the rest of his speech too – his big "tomorrow" speech, therefore, could mean that her death has taken all meaning from his life or his speech could be saying that her life – like his – was meaningless and her death doesn't matter. Ultimately, this is a decision to be made by director, actor and audience together. Yet this line marks the end of the relationship between these two characters – and the true beginning of Macbeth's downfall.

In conclusion, William Shakespeare's "Macbeth" is a play with a key relationship which has a major impact upon the play, both on the narrative of the action but also the mental state of Macbeth himself. Lady Macbeth acts as both a dark shadow of ambition to Macbeth, edging him closer to his own downfall, as well as an example of his guilt and psychological breakdown caused by achieving our deepest and darkest ambitions. This relationship, a tangle of love and power, creates fascinating drama for the audience, with much to teach us about co-dependency and manipulation of our loved ones.

Exemplar Essay 3

Discuss a drama which deals with a major theme (ambition).

William Shakespeare's "Macbeth" is a drama in which there is a theme worthy of discussion, namely the driving force of ambition that dominates this particular drama. The narrative of this play concerns the actions of the Thane Macbeth and his wife Lady Macbeth with the witches leading them to committing the Jacobean sin of regicide and, after this action, both characters then suffer a psychological break down which ultimately leads to their deaths. This essay will focus on the ambition of Macbeth and his wife: how the ambition is seeded and formed; what actions it drives them to carrying out; and the eventual outcome of this ambition and where it leaves the characters.

Shakespeare sets up this theme from the beginning of the play, "Stars, hide your fires! Let not light see my black and deep desires". In Act 1 Scene 4, Macbeth has heard the prophecies of the witches and this has sparked his ambition, his "black and deep desire" to be king. There is a question provoked by the play around the source of this ambition: did the witches bring something hidden to the surface with their prophecy, or did their prophecy put that ambition into Macbeth and it wasn't there before? The audience are left unsure, and in some ways it doesn't matter. It is Macbeth's actions around this ambition that seal his fate as Macbeth knows the quickest (and perhaps only) route to this ambition is to kill Duncan. This is a thought that he should not be having as he is supposed to be the loyal general of the king. Macbeth's ambition is inherently evil, contrary to the idea of the 'divine right of kings' and puts Macbeth and Lady Macbeth in league with the Devil. There is no justification for this ambition – other than self-service. The lack of realism within this ambition can found even in this very opening quotation, with Macbeth shouting exclamations and orders at the "stars" themselves. This sets up the idea of Macbeth being in opposition to the universe and the natural order of all that is good. This quotation is also one of many repeated references to "black" and being hidden. Macbeth wants to "hide" his actions from the "stars" (i.e. heaven and God). He wants to do his deeds unseen and in secret – both because he doesn't want found out but also because he cannot face who he really is. The theme of ambition is implanted within the drama from the very outset, being set up by Shakespeare as a central concern to be followed.

The theme is then developed through the use of a metaphor, "Look like the innocent flower, but be the serpent under it". This is Act 1 Scene 5 and Lady Macbeth has received the news of the prophecies and then greeted Macbeth on his return from war. Lady Macbeth tries to 'sweet talk' Macbeth into committing regicide as she senses Macbeth's ambition already. In this scene it is very clear that Lady Macbeth has abandoned societal expectations (that she be a good wife, meek, subservient to Macbeth and her king) whereas Macbeth is still trying to look like he is holding onto his role as a loyal subject. Lady Macbeth is very overt her about hiding but keeping up appearances ("look like"/"but be") and references the devil ("the serpent"). Serpents also have 'forked tongues' (a metaphor for lying and being manipulative) which is exactly what Lady Macbeth is doing and what she wants Macbeth to do in order to secure their ambition. This quotation clearly establishes that Lady Macbeth has embraced this unholy ambition of theirs, while Macbeth is (or is trying to look like he is) resisting the ambition. Yet there is a sense of 'inevitability' to their giving in to his ambition, which is a polluting force within the drama at this point.

The conclusion to this arc of ambition is described by

Shakespeare in the final Act using a metaphor, "Life's but a walking shadow, a poor player that struts and frets his hour upon the stage, and then is heard no more. It is a tale told by an idiot, full of sound and fury, signifying nothing". This is Macbeth in Act 5, Scene 4 after hearing of the death of Lady Macbeth. Macbeth has truly lost the last person on 'his' side and faces an army of the English (and the rightful King of Scotland) almost totally alone. Ambition has stripped everything from him – while giving him exactly what he wanted. Phrases like "walking shadow" and "poor player" show us that Macbeth has, at this point, given up on the idea of life as a thing of joy or happiness. His ambition has taken these things away from him, He still half-believes (or is pretending to believe) that the witches' prophecies make him unkillable, but he has lost the beauty of life. Macbeth seems to be openly admitting that his time is up ("hour upon the stage" being a short time) and there is a sense of inevitability in this. Finally, Macbeth's ambition has reduced him to thinking of God as an "idiot" telling a "tale" and the pointlessness of his life is "signifying nothing" and full of "fury" and pain. Macbeth's ambition has laid bare the meaningless of all that he has done. The audience can see a broken man on stage, psychologically and spiritually, and the narrative weight of his inevitable defeat weighs heavy on everyone. His dark ambition has led him to a dark end – and there is a sense of narrative rightness and closure to this which is satisfying.

In conclusion, William Shakespeare's "Macbeth" is a play with a key theme which has a major impact upon the play, that being the theme of ambition. Both Macbeth and Lady Macbeth are granted their ambition but, in doing so, lose their sanity, happiness, love and the respect of all around them. It is the classic tale of "be careful what you wish for" in some respects. Shakespeare, ultimately, shows the audience the punishment for overthrowing the rightful, a contextual node to his ruler James 1 who feared being overthrown. Shakespeare shares the lesson that vaulting ambition will lay you low, like Icarus before Macbeth and so many others in literature.

Exemplar Essay 4

Discuss a drama which deals with a major theme (the supernatural).

William Shakespeare's "Macbeth" is a drama in which there is a theme worthy of discussion, namely the grip of the supernatural over the characters and narrative of the play. The narrative of this play concerns the actions of the Thane Macbeth and his wife Lady Macbeth with the witches leading them to committing the Jacobean sin of regicide and, after this action, both characters then suffer a psychological break down which ultimately leads to their deaths. This essay will focus on the ambition of the supernatural, primarily through the characters described in the stage directions as the "Witches". This essay will exam their role in the narrative, their association with their characters and their meaning within the context of the play.

This theme is present from Act 1 Scene 1, the very opening of the play, as seen in Shakespeare's use of alliteration and rhyme, ""Fair is foul, and foul is fair". The witches open up the play, creating a sense of the supernatural and the eerie from the very opening for the audience. Here the witches are discussing the good weather ("fair") versus the terrible events of the battle ("foul") which they are observing. This language is something Lady Macbeth will, later in the play, unconsciously echo. The witches are establishing their own opposition to societal norms – what humans see as "fair" the witches see as "foul", and what humans see as "foul" the witches see as "fair". But Shakespeare is also discussing the difference between appearances and reality (between seeming good and being evil or looking ugly but being good). It establishes, right at the beginning, that you cannot trust what you see on the stage. The supernatural is an unstable arena to exist, a place where everything is not as it seems. It is also a very simple line that, when you investigate it, is almost confusing and strange. Shakespeare is establishing a world where even language is in a state of confusion. The supernatural is here being shown to be a confusing and manipulative realm, a place filled with evil and misunderstanding. This will be born out by the events and actions of the narrative that the witches ignite. The supernatural is not something that can/should be trusted on any level.

Next, the supernatural theme is reflected in the character of Lady Macbeth through the use of a command in Act 1 Scene 5, "Come, you spirits, that tend on moral thoughts! unsex me here, And fill me from the crown to the toe, top-full Of direst cruelty". Lady Macbeth has heard of the prophecies in a letter from Macbeth and has decided she and Macbeth will kill Duncan. Lady Macbeth implies that the supernatural is a constant, surrounding force ("tend on mortal thoughts") like a virus waiting to find its way into the human body. There is no doubt within the play – and within the Jacobean audience – of the unseen world of "spirits" existing and that they are constantly waiting on humans to call upon them. Lady Macbeth seems to be aligning herself with the supernatural, the witches and the Devil to do what must be done (kill Duncan). In fact, her language seems to reflect that of the witches, having a hypnotic spell-like quality as she asks to be changed ("unsex me here") and turned into something more powerful and dangerous. The pervasive presence and temptation of evil and magic is a theme which the Jacobean audience would definitely be familiar with, and Shakespeare writes it into the drama into order to support to biases and interests of James 1, who had a particular fascination with witches and witchcraft. Shakespeare was writing 'for' his intended audience, targeting them with their interests.

The witches make a return to the play near the close,

providing Macbeth with a second round of prophecies, and Shakespeare emphasises their power through the use of child-like rhyme, "Double, double toil and trouble; Fire burn and cauldron bubble". This is Act 4 Scene 1 and is an incredibly famous line, often referenced. Macbeth – no longer sleeping and now losing his mind – goes back to the witches to consult with them. This was a crime in the Jacobean era as it is consulting the devil. The witches are creating a magic brew/spell, speaking in rhyming couplets to create a singsong like effect. It makes the language both very simple but hard to understand. It makes them seem child-like, threatening and inhuman. At its most basic level, the spell brings "toil and trouble", reflecting the basic idea that the supernatural brings nothing good into the world. Another important element here is word choice and repetition. The word "double" is double repeated, showing the importance of doubles. It represents that the witches' words have two meanings (one that Macbeth wants, and the truth), but also represents the play is full of 'double', false or fake people. This is a repeat of the earlier idea of a lack of stability when you invite in the supernatural –when you disrupt the natural order you create an imbalance, inviting disorder. Interestingly, the witches never present themselves as false (they appear as witches) and so, in that sense, are not 'fake' – but they do withhold the truth of in order to sew mischief and discord in the human world. Unlike many of the other characters within the play, the witches between their two scenes have not changed (either for the better or worse), creating a sense of the impervious and immortal to them. The supernatural effects the world but is not affected by it.

In conclusion, William Shakespeare's "Macbeth" is a play with a key theme which has a major impact, the theme of the supernatural. It is the meddling of the witches that begin Macbeth's movement towards his downfall and they then push him to every greater evil. It is the supernatural which Lady Macbeth aligns herself with and, ultimately, abandons her to madness. Shakespeare presents a world where the supernatural is not to be trusted or even interacted with.

Exemplar Essay 5

Discuss a drama with a character you feel sympathy and/or dislike for.

William Shakespeare's "Macbeth" is a drama in which there is a character the audience feels dislike for and sometimes sympathy – this is Macbeth, the titular protagonist. The narrative of this play concerns the actions of the Thane Macbeth and his wife Lady Macbeth with the witches leading them to committing the Jacobean sin of regicide and, after this action, both characters then suffer a psychological break down which ultimately leads to their deaths. This essay will focus on the character of Macbeth and why the audience go through and arc of emotions towards him, from admiration and into dislike and possible sympathy due to his actions and mental state.

In the opening of the drama the audience are supposed to respect and like Macbeth. This can be seen through the writer's use of imagery, "For brave Macbeth — well he deserves that name". Here a wounded solider is baring witness to King Duncan in Act 1 Scene 2 about Macbeth's conduct in winning the battle. Macbeth is described as a formidable soldier and powerfully loyal. The word "brave" is powerful and simple – it sums up Macbeth's prowess in the battlefield. Macbeth is the typical 'Thane' (or Lord) and a paradigm of masculinity and loyalty. This coupled with Lady Macbeth describing him in Act 1 Scene 5 as "too full o' the milk of human kindness" describing him as a good a "kind" man when not in battle as a soldier. Therefore, Macbeth is described as almost the 'perfect' Jacobean man in the opening of the play: a combination of a dangerous solider and a gentle husband. This creates a sympathetic reaction within the audience, which is slightly undercut by the presence and interest of the witches that seems to imply that something else lies under this exterior 'goodness' of Macbeth – something to be afraid of.

This initial impression of Macbeth is immediately undercut by Shakespeare through the use of a metaphor, "Stars, hide your fires! Let not light see my black and deep desires". In Act 1 Scene 4, Macbeth has heard the prophecies of the witches and they have sparked his ambition, his "black and deep desire" to be king. Macbeth knows the quickest (and perhaps only) route to this is to kill Duncan, a thought that he should not be having as he is supposed to be the loyal general of the king. This is one of many repeated references to "black" and being hidden. Macbeth wants to "hide" his actions from the "stars" (i.e. heaven and God). He wants to do his deeds unseen and in secret – both because he doesn't want found out but also because he cannot face who he really is. This begins to create dislike within the audience as we see the burgeoning duplicity of this character who, only a few scenes before, was referred to as "brave" and full of "kindness". We have entered the arc of Macbeth's downfall as a character.

By Act 3, even the remotest respect for Macbeth has collapsed, as reflected by his own use of word choice, ""I am in blood steepp'd in so far, that, should I wade no more, returning were as tedious as go o'er." Macbeth is contemplating the murders he has committed – and the further murders he must commit. He seems contemptable at this point, with the audience feeling an intense dislike for the character. He has risen as a tyrant and a villain. Here he compares these murders to being in water ("wade"). It implies there's so much blood that he is walking in it – literally knee deep. The quotation implies that Macbeth's actions have so much momentum and he has done so much ("steepp'd in so far") that to stop ("wade no more") or go back to his old life ("returning") would be too difficult ("tedious"). It is easier to keep killing. The audience, earlier in the play, may have been hoping for Macbeth's redemption but, by this point, we see only the possibility of his death and downfall – and the audience anticipate it.

This arc of Macbeth's despicability has completed by Act 5 where Shakespeare uses imagery, "Life's but a walking shadow, a poor player that struts and frets his hour upon the stage, and then is heard no more. It is a talk told by an idiot, full of sound and fury, signifying nothing". After the death of Lady Macbeth – but before his own death – Macbeth gives this very famous speech in which he shows he has lost all hope. He believes that God is an "idiot" and life is a "poor player". He sees life as pointless ("signifying nothing") and full of only pain ("full of sound and fury"). Yet still his ambition drives him on to his battle with Macduff – he has come too far to stop now. The sheer collapse of this character, from "brave Macbeth" at the start and even as the villainous but driven character in the middle of the drama, leaves the audience with a sense of unease. Yes, we dislike this character for his action and his own evil, but here is a growing sense of respect or sympathy for his situation and his own collapse. The audience has a sense of sorrow for this character and how much he has changed.

In conclusion, William Shakespeare's "Macbeth" is a play with a powerful character the audience feel a number of emotions towards. We initially feel respect and awe for this solider which the transforms into something like hate and dislike. Yes, this emotion persists even towards the end but there is, at the very end, some sense of sorrow and perhaps even pity what this powerful character has become by the end. We feel the inevitability of his death (there can be no other outcome) but we do feel a sense of sorrow for it. Macbeth can be held up as an example and a lesson – about ambition, about desire, about the effect of the supernatural, and about personal weakness.

Printed in Great Britain
by Amazon